PEGAN DIET

MEGA BUNDLE – 3 Manuscripts in 1 – 120+ Pegan - friendly recipes including Side Dishes, Breakfast, and desserts for a delicious and tasty diet

TABLE OF CONTENTS

This document is geared towards providing exact and reliable information in regards to the topic and issue covered. The publication is sold with the idea that the publisher is not required to render accounting, officially permitted, or otherwise, qualified services. If advice is necessary, legal or professional, a practiced individual in the profession should be ordered.

- From a Declaration of Principles which was accepted and approved equally by a Committee of the American Bar Association and a Committee of Publishers and Associations.

Introduction

Pegan recipes for personal enjoyment but also for family enjoyment.
You will love them for sure for how easy it is to prepare them.

BREAKFAST

BLUEBERRY PANCAKES

Serves: **4**

Prep Time: **10**   Minutes

Cook Time: **20**   Minutes

Total Time: **30**   Minutes

INGREDIENTS

- 1 cup whole wheat flour
- ¼ tsp baking soda
- ¼ tsp baking powder
- 1 cup blueberries
- 2 eggs
- 1 cup milk

DIRECTIONS

1. In a bowl combine all ingredients together and mix well
2. In a skillet heat olive oil
3. Pour ¼ of the batter and cook each pancake for 1-2 minutes per side
4. When ready remove from heat and serve

Serves: **4**

Prep Time: **10**   Minutes

Cook Time: **30**   Minutes

Total Time: **40**   Minutes

INGREDIENTS

- 1 cup whole wheat flour
- ¼ tsp baking soda
- ¼ tsp baking powder
- 1 cup apples
- 2 eggs
- 1 cup milk

DIRECTIONS

1. In a bowl combine all ingredients together and mix well
2. In a skillet heat olive oil
3. Pour ¼ of the batter and cook each pancake for 1-2 minutes per side
4. When ready remove from heat and serve

BANANA PANCAKES

Serves: **4**
Prep Time: **10** Minutes

Cook Time: **20** Minutes

Total Time: **30** Minutes

INGREDIENTS

- 1 cup whole wheat flour
- ¼ tsp baking soda
- ¼ tsp baking powder
- 1 cup mashed banana
- 2 eggs
- 1 cup milk

DIRECTIONS

1. In a bowl combine all ingredients together and mix well
2. In a skillet heat olive oil
3. Pour ¼ of the batter and cook each pancake for 1-2 minutes per side
4. When ready remove from heat and serve

Serves: **4**

Prep Time: **10**   Minutes

Cook Time: **20**   Minutes

Total Time: **30**   Minutes

INGREDIENTS

- 1 cup whole wheat flour
- ¼ tsp baking soda
- ¼ tsp baking powder
- 1 cup apricots
- 2 eggs
- 1 cup milk

DIRECTIONS

1. In a bowl combine all ingredients together and mix well
2. In a skillet heat olive oil
3. Pour ¼ of the batter and cook each pancake for 1-2 minutes per side
4. When ready remove from heat and serve

PANCAKES

Serves: **4**

Prep Time: **10** Minutes

Cook Time: **30** Minutes

Total Time: **40** Minutes

INGREDIENTS

- 1 cup whole wheat flour
- ¼ tsp baking soda
- ¼ tsp baking powder
- 2 eggs
- 1 cup milk

DIRECTIONS

1. In a bowl combine all ingredients together and mix well
2. In a skillet heat olive oil
3. Pour ¼ of the batter and cook each pancake for 1-2 minutes per side
4. When ready remove from heat and serve

Serves: **8-12**
Prep Time: **10**   Minutes

Cook Time: **20**   Minutes

Total Time: **30**   Minutes

INGREDIENTS

- 2 eggs
- 1 tablespoon olive oil
- 1 cup milk
- 2 cups whole wheat flour
- 1 tsp baking soda
- ¼ tsp baking soda
- 1 tsp ginger
- ½ cup cranberries
- ¼ cup molasses

DIRECTIONS

1. In a bowl combine all wet ingredients
2. In another bowl combine all dry ingredients
3. Combine wet and dry ingredients together
4. Pour mixture into 8-12 prepared muffin cups, fill 2/3 of the cups
5. Bake for 18-20 minutes at 375 F

DURIAN MUFFINS

Serves:	*8-12*	
Prep Time:	*10*	Minutes
Cook Time:	*20*	Minutes
Total Time:	*30*	Minutes

INGREDIENTS

- 2 eggs
- 1 tablespoon olive oil
- 1 cup milk
- 2 cups whole wheat flour
- 1 tsp baking soda
- ¼ tsp baking soda
- 1 tsp cinnamon
- 1 cup durian

DIRECTIONS

1. In a bowl combine all wet ingredients
2. In another bowl combine all dry ingredients
3. Combine wet and dry ingredients together
4. Pour mixture into 8-12 prepared muffin cups, fill 2/3 of the cups
5. Bake for 18-20 minutes at 375 F
6. When ready remove from the oven and serve

Serves: *8-12*
Prep Time: *10*   Minutes

Cook Time: *20*   Minutes

Total Time: *30*   Minutes

INGREDIENTS

- 2 eggs
- 1 tablespoon olive oil
- 1 cup milk
- 2 cups whole wheat flour
- 1 tsp baking soda
- ¼ tsp baking soda
- 1 tsp cinnamon
- 1 cup blueberries

DIRECTIONS

1. In a bowl combine all wet ingredients
2. In another bowl combine all dry ingredients
3. Combine wet and dry ingredients together
4. Fold in blueberries and mix well
5. Pour mixture into 8-12 prepared muffin cups, fill 2/3 of the cups
6. Bake for 18-20 minutes at 375 F

FEIJOA MUFFINS

Serves: **8-12**

Prep Time: **10** Minutes

Cook Time: **20** Minutes

Total Time: **30** Minutes

INGREDIENTS

- 2 eggs
- 1 tablespoon olive oil
- 1 cup milk
- 2 cups whole wheat flour
- 1 tsp baking soda
- ¼ tsp baking soda
- 1 tsp cinnamon
- 1 cup feijoa

DIRECTIONS

1. In a bowl combine all wet ingredients
2. In another bowl combine all dry ingredients
3. Combine wet and dry ingredients together
4. Pour mixture into 8-12 prepared muffin cups, fill 2/3 of the cups
5. Bake for 18-20 minutes at 375 F
6. When ready remove from the oven and serve

KIWI MUFFINS

Serves:	8-12	
Prep Time:	10	Minutes
Cook Time:	20	Minutes
Total Time:	30	Minutes

INGREDIENTS

- 2 eggs
- 1 tablespoon olive oil
- 1 cup milk
- 2 cups whole wheat flour
- 1 tsp baking soda
- ¼ tsp baking soda
- 1 tsp cinnamon
- 1 cup kiwi

DIRECTIONS

1. In a bowl combine all wet ingredients
2. In another bowl combine all dry ingredients
3. Combine wet and dry ingredients together
4. Pour mixture into 8-12 prepared muffin cups, fill 2/3 of the cups
5. Bake for 18-20 minutes at 375 F
6. When ready remove from the oven and serve

MUFFINS

Serves: **8-12**

Prep Time: **10** Minutes

Cook Time: **20** Minutes

Total Time: **30** Minutes

INGREDIENTS

- 2 eggs
- 1 tablespoon olive oil
- 1 cup milk
- 2 cups whole wheat flour
- 1 tsp baking soda
- ¼ tsp baking soda
- 1 tsp cinnamon

DIRECTIONS

1. In a bowl combine all wet ingredients
2. In another bowl combine all dry ingredients
3. Combine wet and dry ingredients together
4. Pour mixture into 8-12 prepared muffin cups, fill 2/3 of the cups
5. Bake for 18-20 minutes at 375 F
6. When ready remove from the oven and serve

GOAT CHEESE OMELETTE

Serves: *1*

Prep Time: *5*   Minutes

Cook Time: *10*   Minutes

Total Time: *15*   Minutes

INGREDIENTS

- 2 eggs
- ¼ tsp salt
- ¼ tsp black pepper
- 1 tablespoon olive oil
- ¼ cup goat cheese
- ¼ tsp basil

DIRECTIONS

1. In a bowl combine all ingredients together and mix well
2. In a skillet heat olive oil and pour the egg mixture
3. Cook for 1-2 minutes per side
4. When ready remove omelette from the skillet and serve

BACON OMELETTE

Serves: **1**

Prep Time: **5**   Minutes

Cook Time: **10**   Minutes

Total Time: **15**   Minutes

INGREDIENTS

- 2 eggs
- ¼ tsp salt
- ¼ tsp black pepper
- 1 tablespoon olive oil
- ½ cup bacon
- ¼ tsp basil
- 1 cup zucchini

DIRECTIONS

1. In a bowl combine all ingredients together and mix well
2. In a skillet heat olive oil and pour the egg mixture
3. Cook for 1-2 minutes per side
4. When ready remove omelette from the skillet and serve

ONION OMELETTE

Serves: **1**

Prep Time: **5**   Minutes

Cook Time: **10**   Minutes

Total Time: **15**   Minutes

INGREDIENTS

- 2 eggs
- ¼ tsp salt
- ¼ tsp black pepper
- 1 tablespoon olive oil
- ¼ cup cheese
- ¼ tsp basil
- 1 cup red onion

DIRECTIONS

1. In a bowl combine all ingredients together and mix well
2. In a skillet heat olive oil and pour the egg mixture
3. Cook for 1-2 minutes per side
4. When ready remove omelette from the skillet and serve

FETA CHEESE OMELETTE

Serves: *1*
Prep Time: *5*   Minutes
Cook Time: *10* Minutes
Total Time: *15* Minutes

INGREDIENTS

- 2 eggs
- ¼ tsp salt
- ¼ tsp black pepper
- 1 tablespoon olive oil
- ¼ cup cheese
- ¼ tsp basil
- ½ cup feta cheese

DIRECTIONS

1. In a bowl combine all ingredients together and mix well
2. In a skillet heat olive oil and pour the egg mixture
3. Cook for 1-2 minutes per side
4. When ready remove omelette from the skillet and serve

TOMATO OMELETTE

Serves: **1**
Prep Time: **5**   Minutes

Cook Time: **10**   Minutes

Total Time: **15**   Minutes

INGREDIENTS

- 2 eggs
- ¼ tsp salt
- ¼ tsp black pepper
- 1 tablespoon olive oil
- ¼ cup cheese
- ¼ tsp basil
- 1 cup tomatoes

DIRECTIONS

1. In a bowl combine all ingredients together and mix well
2. In a skillet heat olive oil and pour the egg mixture
3. Cook for 1-2 minutes per side
4. When ready remove omelette from the skillet and serve

BEANS OMELETTE

Serves: **1**

Prep Time: **5**   Minutes

Cook Time: **10**   Minutes

Total Time: **15**   Minutes

INGREDIENTS

- 2 eggs
- ¼ tsp salt
- ¼ tsp black pepper
- 1 tablespoon olive oil
- ¼ cup cheese
- ¼ tsp basil
- 1 cup beans

DIRECTIONS

1. In a bowl combine all ingredients together and mix well
2. In a skillet heat olive oil and pour the egg mixture
3. Cook for 1-2 minutes per side
4. When ready remove omelette from the skillet and serve

BREAKFAST GRANOLA

Serves: 2

Prep Time: 5   Minutes

Cook Time: 30   Minutes

Total Time: 35   Minutes

INGREDIENTS

- 1 tsp vanilla extract
- 1 tablespoon honey
- 1 lb. rolled oats
- 2 tablespoons sesame seeds
- ¼ lb. almonds
- ¼ lb. berries

DIRECTIONS

1. Preheat the oven to 325 F
2. Spread the granola onto a baking sheet
3. Bake for 12-15 minutes, remove and mix everything
4. Bake for another 12-15 minutes or until slightly brown
5. When ready remove from the oven and serve

BLUEBERRY PANCAKES

Serves: **4**
Prep Time: **10**   Minutes

Cook Time: **20**   Minutes

Total Time: **30**   Minutes

INGREDIENTS

- 1 cup whole wheat flour
- ¼ tsp baking soda
- ¼ tsp baking powder
- 1 cup blueberries
- 2 eggs
- 1 cup milk

DIRECTIONS

1. In a bowl combine all ingredients together and mix well
2. In a skillet heat olive oil
3. Pour ¼ of the batter and cook each pancake for 1-2 minutes per side
4. When ready remove from heat and serve

APPLE PANCAKES

Serves: **4**
Prep Time: **10**   Minutes

Cook Time: **30**   Minutes

Total Time: **40**   Minutes

INGREDIENTS

- 1 cup whole wheat flour
- ¼ tsp baking soda
- ¼ tsp baking powder
- 1 cup apples
- 2 eggs
- 1 cup milk

DIRECTIONS

1. In a bowl combine all ingredients together and mix well
2. In a skillet heat olive oil
3. Pour ¼ of the batter and cook each pancake for 1-2 minutes per side
4. When ready remove from heat and serve

BANANA PANCAKES

Serves: **4**

Prep Time: **10** Minutes

Cook Time: **20** Minutes

Total Time: **30** Minutes

INGREDIENTS

- 1 cup whole wheat flour
- ¼ tsp baking soda
- ¼ tsp baking powder
- 1 cup mashed banana
- 2 eggs
- 1 cup milk

DIRECTIONS

1. In a bowl combine all ingredients together and mix well
2. In a skillet heat olive oil
3. Pour ¼ of the batter and cook each pancake for 1-2 minutes per side
4. When ready remove from heat and serve

APRICOTS PANCAKES

Serves: **4**

Prep Time: **10**   Minutes

Cook Time: **20**   Minutes

Total Time: **30**   Minutes

INGREDIENTS

- 1 cup whole wheat flour
- ¼ tsp baking soda
- ¼ tsp baking powder
- 1 cup apricots
- 2 eggs
- 1 cup milk

DIRECTIONS

1. In a bowl combine all ingredients together and mix well
2. In a skillet heat olive oil
3. Pour ¼ of the batter and cook each pancake for 1-2 minutes per side
4. When ready remove from heat and serve

PANCAKES

Serves: **4**

Prep Time: **10**   Minutes

Cook Time: **30**   Minutes

Total Time: **40**   Minutes

INGREDIENTS

- 1 cup whole wheat flour
- ¼ tsp baking soda
- ¼ tsp baking powder
- 2 eggs
- 1 cup milk

DIRECTIONS

1. In a bowl combine all ingredients together and mix well
2. In a skillet heat olive oil
3. Pour ¼ of the batter and cook each pancake for 1-2 minutes per side
4. When ready remove from heat and serve

RAISIN BREAKFAST MIX

Serves: *1*
Prep Time: 5   Minutes

Cook Time: 5   Minutes

Total Time: *10*   Minutes

INGREDIENTS

- ½ cup dried raisins
- ½ cup dried pecans
- ¼ cup almonds
- 1 cup coconut milk
- 1 tsp cinnamon

DIRECTIONS

1. In a bowl combine all ingredients together
2. Serve with milk

SAUSAGE BREAKFAST SANDWICH

Serves: 2
Prep Time: 5   Minutes
Cook Time: 15   Minutes
Total Time: 20   Minutes

INGREDIENTS

- ¼ cup egg substitute
- 1 muffin
- 1 turkey sausage patty
- 1 tablespoon cheddar cheese

DIRECTIONS

1. In a skillet pour egg and cook on low heat
2. Place turkey sausage patty in a pan and cook for 4-5 minutes per side
3. On a toasted muffin place the cooked egg, top with a sausage patty and cheddar cheese
4. Serve when ready

BREAKFAST COOKIES

Serves: **8-12**

Prep Time: **5**   Minutes

Cook Time: **15**   Minutes

Total Time: **20**   Minutes

INGREDIENTS

- 1 cup rolled oats
- ¼ cup applesauce
- ½ tsp vanilla extract
- 3 tablespoons chocolate chips
- 2 tablespoons dried fruits
- 1 tsp cinnamon

DIRECTIONS

1. Preheat the oven to 325 F
2. In a bowl combine all ingredients together and mix well
3. Scoop cookies using an ice cream scoop
4. Place cookies onto a prepared baking sheet
5. Place in the oven for 12-15 minutes or until the cookies are done
6. When ready remove from the oven and serve

PEAR TART

Serves: *6-8*

Prep Time: 25   Minutes

Cook Time: 25   Minutes

Total Time: *50*   Minutes

INGREDIENTS

- 1 lb. pears
- 2 oz. brown sugar
- ½ lb. flaked almonds
- ¼ lb. porridge oat
- 2 oz. flour
- ¼ lb. almonds
- pastry sheets
- 2 tablespoons syrup

DIRECTIONS

1. Preheat oven to 400 F, unfold pastry sheets and place them on a baking sheet
2. Toss together all ingredients together and mix well
3. Spread mixture in a single layer on the pastry sheets
4. Before baking decorate with your desired fruits
5. Bake at 400 F for 22-25 minutes or until golden brown
6. When ready remove from the oven and serve

CARDAMOM TART

Serves: *6-8*
Prep Time: 25   Minutes

Cook Time: 25   Minutes

Total Time: *50*   Minutes

INGREDIENTS

- 4-5 pears
- 2 tablespoons lemon juice
- pastry sheets

CARDAMOM FILLING

- ½ lb. butter
- ½ lb. brown sugar
- ½ lb. almonds
- ¼ lb. flour
- 1 ¼ tsp cardamom
- 2 eggs

DIRECTIONS

1. Preheat oven to 400 F, unfold pastry sheets and place them on a baking sheet
2. Toss together all ingredients together and mix well
3. Spread mixture in a single layer on the pastry sheets
4. Before baking decorate with your desired fruits

5. Bake at 400 F for 22-25 minutes or until golden brown
6. When ready remove from the oven and serve

APPLE TART

Serves: *6-8*

Prep Time: 25   Minutes

Cook Time: 25   Minutes

Total Time: *50*   Minutes

INGREDIENTS

- pastry sheets

FILLING

- 1 tsp lemon juice
- 3 oz. brown sugar
- 1 lb. apples
- 150 ml double cream
- 2 eggs

DIRECTIONS

1. Preheat oven to 400 F, unfold pastry sheets and place them on a baking sheet
2. Toss together all ingredients together and mix well
3. Spread mixture in a single layer on the pastry sheets
4. Before baking decorate with your desired fruits
5. Bake at 400 F for 22-25 minutes or until golden brown
6. When ready remove from the oven and serve

SMOOTHIES AND DRINKS

BANANA BREAKFAST SMOOTHIE

Serves: *1*
Prep Time: *5*   Minutes

Cook Time: *5*   Minutes

Total Time: *10*   Minutes

INGREDIENTS

- ½ cup vanilla yogurt
- 2 tsp honey
- Pinch of cinnamon
- 1 banana
- 1 cup ice

DIRECTIONS

1. In a blender place all ingredients and blend until smooth
2. Pour the smoothie in a glass and serve

Serves: *1*
Prep Time: 5   Minutes

Cook Time: 5   Minutes

Total Time: *10*   Minutes

INGREDIENTS

- 1 cup soy milk
- 1 banana
- 1 tablespoon vanilla essence
- 1 cup strawberries
- ¼ tsp cinnamon

DIRECTIONS

1. In a blender place all ingredients and blend until smooth
2. Pour smoothie in a glass and serve

PEANUT BUTTER SMOOTHIE

Serves: **1**

Prep Time: **5**   Minutes

Cook Time: **5**   Minutes

Total Time: **10**   Minutes

INGREDIENTS

- 1 cup soy milk
- 1 banana
- 1 tablespoon peanut butter
- ¼ tsp cinnamon
- 1 cup ice

DIRECTIONS

1. In a blender place all ingredients and blend until smooth
2. Pour smoothie in a glass and serve

Serves: *1*
Prep Time: *5*   Minutes

Cook Time: *5*   Minutes

Total Time: *10* Minutes

INGREDIENTS

- 1 banana
- 1 cup ice
- ¼ cup blueberries
- 1 cup spinach

DIRECTIONS

1. In a blender place all ingredients and blend until smooth
2. Pour smoothie in a glass and serve

STRAWBERRY SMOOTHIE

Serves: *1*
Prep Time: 5   Minutes

Cook Time: 5   Minutes

Total Time: *10*   Minutes

INGREDIENTS

- 1 cup strawberries
- 1 cup cranberry juice
- ½ cup orange juice
- 1 cup vanilla yogurt

DIRECTIONS

1. In a blender place all ingredients and blend until smooth
2. Pour smoothie in a glass and serve

Serves: **1**

Prep Time: **5** Minutes

Cook Time: **5** Minutes

Total Time: **10** Minutes

INGREDIENTS

- 2 bananas
- 2 tablespoons cocoa powder
- 1 tablespoon maple syrup
- ½ cup peanut butter
- 1 cup ice
- 2 cups almond milk

DIRECTIONS

1. In a blender place all ingredients and blend until smooth
2. Pour smoothie in a glass and serve

AVOCADO SMOOTHIE

Serves: **1**
Prep Time: **5**   Minutes

Cook Time: **5**   Minutes

Total Time: **10** Minutes

INGREDIENTS

- 1 avocado
- 2 cups mango juice
- 1 cup orange juice
- 1 cup ice

DIRECTIONS

1. In a blender place all ingredients and blend until smooth
2. Pour smoothie in a glass and serve

Serves: **1**

Prep Time: **5**   Minutes

Cook Time: **5**   Minutes

Total Time: **10** Minutes

INGREDIENTS

- 1 cup tomato juice
- ½ cup carrot juice
- 1 celery
- 1 cup spinach
- 1 cucumber
- 1 cup ice

DIRECTIONS

1. In a blender place all ingredients and blend until smooth
2. Pour smoothie in a glass and serve

BERRY SMOOTHIE

Serves: *1*
Prep Time: 5   Minutes

Cook Time: 5   Minutes

Total Time: *10*   Minutes

INGREDIENTS

- 1 cup strawberries
- 1 cup blueberries
- 1 cup yogurt
- 1 cup beet juice
- 1 cup ice

DIRECTIONS

1. In a blender place all ingredients and blend until smooth
2. Pour smoothie in a glass and serve

CARDAMOM SMOOTHIE

Serves: **1**

Prep Time: **5**   Minutes

Cook Time: **5**   Minutes

Total Time: **10**   Minutes

INGREDIENTS

- 1 banana
- 2 dates
- 1 cup Greek yogurt
- 1-inch ginger
- ½ cup coconut milk
- ½ tsp cardamom

DIRECTIONS

1. In a blender place all ingredients and blend until smooth
2. Pour smoothie in a glass and serve

SECOND COOKBOOK

MUSHROOM OMELETTE

Serves: **1**

Prep Time: **5** Minutes

Cook Time: **10** Minutes

Total Time: **15** Minutes

INGREDIENTS

- 2 eggs
- ¼ tsp salt
- ¼ tsp black pepper
- 1 tablespoon olive oil
- ¼ cup cheese
- ¼ tsp basil
- 1 cup mushrooms

DIRECTIONS

1. In a bowl combine all ingredients together and mix well
2. In a skillet heat olive oil and pour the egg mixture
3. Cook for 1-2 minutes per side
4. When ready remove omelette from the skillet and serve

Serves: **2**

Prep Time: **10** Minutes

Cook Time: **10** Minutes

Total Time: **20** Minutes

INGREDIENTS

- 2 eggs
- pinch of salt
- 1 tablespoon chives
- 1 tablespoon pesto
- bit of goat cheese
- handful of salad greens

DIRECTIONS

1. In a bowl beat eggs and pour in a skillet over medium heat, sprinkle with chives, and spread the pesto across the omelette
2. Sprinkle salad greens, cheese and season with salt

Serves: **6**
Prep Time: **10**   Minutes

Cook Time: **10**   Minutes

Total Time: **20**   Minutes

INGREDIENTS

- ½ cup quinoa
- 1 tablespoon olive oil
- 1 onion
- 3 cups spinach leaves
- 1 garlic clove
- ¼ shallot
- salt
- ¼ cup cheddar cheese
- ¼ cup parmesan cheese
- 1 egg

DIRECTIONS

1. Preheat oven to 350 F and line a six-cup muffin pan
2. Combine water and quinoa in a saucepan and bring to boil
3. Lower the heat and cook for 12-15 minutes, remove from heat and allow to cool
4. In a skillet heat oil, add onion and cook for 4-5 minutes

5. Stir in shallot, garlic and spinach and season with salt and pepper
6. Remove the pan from heat and mix with quinoa, pour in the eggs
7. Divide the batter into muffin cups and bake for 30-35 minutes

Serves: **4**
Prep Time: **10** Minutes

Cook Time: **10** Minutes

Total Time: **20** Minutes

INGREDIENTS

- **10 cups**
- **½ cup butter**
- **1 cup diced celery**
- **¼ cup onion**
- **1 cup chopped cranberries**
- **½ cup sugar**
- **1 tsp sage**
- **1 tsp rosemary**
- **1 tsp sage**
- **1 tsp rosemary**
- **1 tsp thyme**
- **½ cup parsley**
- **salt**
- **1 lb. ground sausage**
- **1 cup chicken broth**

DIRECTIONS

1. In a saucepan heat butter over medium heat, add onion, celery and cook, add cranberries, sage, sugar, rosemary, parsley, thyme
2. Season with salt and pepper
3. Brown the sausage in a skillet, drain off fat
4. Toss the ingredients in the bowl and add chicken broth
5. Serve when ready

Serves: **6**
Prep Time: **10**   Minutes

Cook Time: **10**   Minutes

Total Time: **20**   Minutes

INGREDIENTS

- 10 oz. chopped kale
- 2 eggs
- 2 egg whites
- ½ cup leek
- ½ cup chopped tomato
- ½ cup bell pepper

DIRECTIONS

1. Preheat oven to 325 F and line a muffin pan with paper liners
2. In a bowl leek, egg whites, tomatoes, kale, eggs and bell pepper
3. Divide mixture into muffin cups and bake for 15-20 minutes
4. Remove and serve

Serves: **6**

Prep Time: **10** Minutes

Cook Time: **10** Minutes

Total Time: **20** Minutes

INGREDIENTS

- 3 ears corn
- 1 tablespoon lemon zest
- 1 tablespoon lemon juice
- ½ cup butter
- 1 tablespoon honey
- ¼ tsp salt
- ½ tsp pepper
- 1 cup quinoa
- 3 scallions

DIRECTIONS

1. In a pot place the corn and fill the pan with water, bring to boil and cover for 5-6 minutes
2. Remove from pot and let it cool
3. In a bowl mix the rest of the ingredients for dressing: lemon juice, melted butter, lemon zest, honey, pepper

4. Cook the quinoa in a pot, add scallions in a bowl with the dressing and toss well
5. Season with salt and serve

BERRY GRANOLA

Serves: **4**
Prep Time: **10**   Minutes

Cook Time: **10**   Minutes

Total Time: **20**   Minutes

INGREDIENTS

- **2 tablespoons chia**
- **¾ cup rolled oats**
- **1 cup vanilla cashewmilk**
- **½ cup fresh blueberries**
- **2 strawberries**
- **½ raspberries**
- **sprinkle of granola**

DIRECTIONS

1. **In a bowl mix cashewmilk, oats, chia and divide into 2 servings**
2. **Refrigerate overnight, remove top with berries and serve**

Serves: **2**
Prep Time: **5**   Minutes

Cook Time: **5**   Minutes

Total Time: **10**   Minutes

INGREDIENTS

- 2 tablespoons chia
- ¾ cup rolled oats
- 1 cup vanilla cashewmilk
- ¼ cup peach
- ¼ plum
- 3 basil leaves
- 1 tsp pumpkin seeds
- 1 tsp hemp seeds

DIRECTIONS

1. In a bowl mix cashewmilk, oats, chia and oats, divide into 2-3 servings
2. Refrigerate overnight
3. Remove and serve

AVOCADO BROWNIE

Serves: **4**

Prep Time: **10** Minutes

Cook Time: **30** Minutes

Total Time: **40** Minutes

INGREDIENTS

- 1 ripe avocado
- 3 tablespoons melted butter
- 1 egg
- ¼ cup brown sugar
- ¼ maple syrup
- 1 tablespoon vanilla extract
- ¾ cup cocoa powder
- ½ tsp salt
- ½ cup gluten-free flour
- ¼ cup dark chocolate chips

DIRECTIONS

1. Preheat the oven to 325 F
2. In a bowl mash the avocado, brown sugar, maple syrup, vanilla, sugar, water, butter, add cocoa powder
3. In a bowl mix salt and flour and stir in avocado mixture, spread bake in the pan and bake for 35 minutes

4. Remove and cool before serving

Serves: *1*
Prep Time: 5   Minutes

Cook Time: 5   Minutes

Total Time: *10* Minutes

INGREDIENTS

- 1 cup corn cereal
- 1 cup rice cereal
- ¼ cup cocoa cereal
- ¼ cup rice cakes

DIRECTIONS

1. **In a bowl combine all ingredients together**
2. **Serve with milk**

Serves: 2

Prep Time: 5   Minutes

Cook Time: 15   Minutes

Total Time: 20   Minutes

INGREDIENTS

- ¼ cup egg substitute
- 1 muffin
- 1 turkey sausage patty
- 1 tablespoon cheddar cheese

DIRECTIONS

1. In a skillet pour egg and cook on low heat
2. Place turkey sausage patty in a pan and cook for 4-5 minutes per side
3. On a toasted muffin place the cooked egg, top with a sausage patty and cheddar cheese
4. Serve when ready

BREAKFAST GRANOLA

Serves: 2
Prep Time: 5   Minutes
Cook Time: 30   Minutes
Total Time: 35   Minutes

INGREDIENTS

- 1 tsp vanilla extract
- 1 tablespoon honey
- 1 lb. rolled oats
- 2 tablespoons sesame seeds
- ¼ lb. almonds
- ¼ lb. berries

DIRECTIONS

1. Preheat the oven to 325 F
2. Spread the granola onto a baking sheet
3. Bake for 12-15 minutes, remove and mix everything
4. Bake for another 12-15 minutes or until slightly brown
5. When ready remove from the oven and serve

RASPBERRY CRUMBLE

Serves: *4*
Prep Time: *10*   Minutes

Cook Time: *50*   Minutes

Total Time: *60*   Minutes

INGREDIENTS

- 2 eggs
- 1 cup raspberries
- 1 cup apple juice
- 1 cup oats
- 1 tablespoon butter
- 1 tablespoon brown sugar
- 1 tablespoon cinnamon
- ¼ tsp cloves

DIRECTIONS

1. Preheat oven to 375 F
2. In a bowl combine raspberries, apple slices and apple juice
3. In another bowl combine sugar, spices, oats, butter and mix well
4. Cover apple slices with crumble topping
5. Bake for 45-50 minutes
6. When ready remove and serve

QUINOA CREPES WITH APPLESAUCE

Serves: **4**

Prep Time: **10** Minutes

Cook Time: **30** Minutes

Total Time: **40** Minutes

INGREDIENTS

- 1 cup quinoa flour
- ½ cup tapioca flour
- 1 tsp baking soda
- 1 tsp cinnamon
- 1 cup water
- 2 tablespoons canola oil
- 2 cups organic apple sauce

DIRECTIONS

1. In a bowl combine quinoa flour, baking soda, cinnamon, tapioca flour, water, oil and whisk well
2. Preheat a skillet over medium heat and pour ¼ cup batter into skillet
3. Cook each crepe on low heat for 1-2 minutes per side
4. When ready remove and serve with apple sauce

CHEESE OMELETTE

Serves: **1**

Prep Time: **5**   Minutes

Cook Time: **10**   Minutes

Total Time: **15**   Minutes

INGREDIENTS

- 2 eggs
- ¼ tsp salt
- ¼ tsp black pepper
- 1 tablespoon olive oil
- ¼ cup cheese
- ¼ tsp basil
- 1 cup low-fat cheese

DIRECTIONS

1. In a bowl combine all ingredients together and mix well
2. In a skillet heat olive oil and pour the egg mixture
3. Cook for 1-2 minutes per side
4. When ready remove omelette from the skillet and serve

CUCUMBER OMELETTE

Serves: **1**

Prep Time: **5** Minutes

Cook Time: **10** Minutes

Total Time: **15** Minutes

INGREDIENTS

- 2 eggs
- ¼ tsp salt
- ¼ tsp black pepper
- 1 tablespoon olive oil
- ¼ cup cheese
- ¼ tsp basil
- 1 cup cucumber

DIRECTIONS

1. In a bowl combine all ingredients together and mix well
2. In a skillet heat olive oil and pour the egg mixture
3. Cook for 1-2 minutes per side
4. When ready remove omelette from the skillet and serve

PANCAKES

BANANA PANCAKES

Serves: **4**
Prep Time: **10** Minutes

Cook Time: **20** Minutes

Total Time: **30** Minutes

INGREDIENTS

- 1 cup whole wheat flour
- ¼ tsp baking soda
- ¼ tsp baking powder
- 1 cup mashed banana
- 2 eggs
- 1 cup milk

DIRECTIONS

1. In a bowl combine all ingredients together and mix well
2. In a skillet heat olive oil
3. Pour ¼ of the batter and cook each pancake for 1-2 minutes per side
4. When ready remove from heat and serve

BUCKWHEAT PANCAKES

Serves: **6**

Prep Time: **5**   Minutes

Cook Time: **10**   Minutes

Total Time: **15**   Minutes

INGREDIENTS

- **1 cup buckwheat flour**
- **1 tablespoon brown sugar**
- **¼ tsp salt**
- **1 tsp baking powder**
- **1 cup almond milk**
- **1 tablespoon canola oil**
- **2 bananas**

DIRECTIONS

1. **In a bowl combine dry ingredients**
2. **Add wet ingredients and mix well**
3. **In a skillet pour ¼ cup batter and cook for 1-2 minutes per side**
4. **When ready remove and serve with syrup**

MORNING COOKIES

Serves: **6**
Prep Time: **10**   Minutes

Cook Time: **15**   Minutes

Total Time: **25**   Minutes

INGREDIENTS

- **3 bananas**
- **¼ cup peanut butter**
- **¼ cup cocoa powder**
- **handful of salt**

DIRECTIONS

1. **Preheat oven to 325 F**
2. **In a bowl mix all ingredients**
3. **Form small cookies and place them onto a greased cookie sheet**
4. **Sprinkle with salt and bake for 12-15 minutes**
5. **Remove and serve**

BLUEBERRY BITES

Serves: *8*
Prep Time: *5*   Minutes

Cook Time: *30* Minutes

Total Time: *35* Minutes

INGREDIENTS

- **2 cups oats**
- **½ tsp cinnamon**
- **1 cup blueberries**
- **½ cup honey**
- **½ cup almond butter**
- **1 tsp vanilla**

DIRECTIONS

1. **Mix all of the ingredients together, except for the blueberries.**
2. **Fold in the blueberries and refrigerate for 30 minutes.**
3. **Form balls from the mixture and serve.**

Serves: *8*
Prep Time: 5   Minutes

Cook Time: *10*   Minutes

Total Time: *15*   Minutes

INGREDIENTS

- **1/3 cup honey**
- **4 lemons juice**
- **Ice**
- **4 strips of lemon peel**
- **2 tbs ginger root**
- **2 sprigs rosemary**

DIRECTIONS

1. **Mix the honey, ginger, lemon peel and 2 sprigs rosemary in a pot with 2 cups water.**
2. **Bring to a boil, then simmer for 10 minutes.**
3. **Remove from heat and allow to cool for 15 minutes.**
4. **Strain into a pitcher.**
5. **Discard the ginger and rosemary.**
6. **Add 6 cups of cold water and lemon juice to the pitcher.**
7. **Stir to combine and serve with ice.**

LIME GRILLED CORN

Serves: **4**
Prep Time: **5**   Minutes

Cook Time: **15**   Minutes

Total Time: **20**   Minutes

INGREDIENTS

- **4 corns**
- **2 tbs mayonnaise**
- **Salt**
- **Pepper**
- **2 tbs lime juice**
- **¼ tsp chili powder**

DIRECTIONS

1. Preheat the grill.
2. Cook the shucked corn onto the grill for 5 minutes.
3. Turn every few minutes until all sides are charred.
4. Mix the mayonnaise, chili powder, and lime juice in a bowl.
5. Season with salt and pepper and add lime juice and chili powder.
6. Serve coated with the mayonnaise mixture.

Serves: **6**
Prep Time: **10**   Minutes

Cook Time: **30**   Minutes

Total Time: **40**   Minutes

INGREDIENTS

- **4 apples**
- **2 tsp cinnamon**
- **1 cup flour**
- **½ cup walnuts**
- **2 cups quinoa**
- **1/3 cup ground almonds**

DIRECTIONS

1. **Preheat the oven to 350F.**
2. **Oil a baking dish.**
3. **Place the apples into prepared dishes.**
4. **Mix the remaining ingredients in a bowl.**
5. **Crumble over the apples.**
6. **Bake for 30 minutes.**
7. **Serve immediately.**

Serves: **18**

Prep Time: **10**   Minutes

Cook Time: **10**   Minutes

Total Time: **20**   Minutes

INGREDIENTS

- 1 ¾ cups flour
- 1 ¾ ground ginger
- ¼ tsp ground cinnamon
- 1/8 tsp nutmeg
- 1/8 tsp cloves
- 1 ½ tsp cornstarch
- ¼ cup milk
- ¼ cup molasses
- 3 tbs Swerve
- ¼ tsp salt
- 2 tbs butter
- 1 egg white
- 2 ¼ tsp vanilla
- 2 tsp stevia
- 1 tsp baking powder

DIRECTIONS

1. Preheat the oven to 325F.
2. Mix the cornstarch, nutmeg, flour, cloves, ginger, cinnamon, baking powder, and salt in a bowl.
3. In another bowl, whisk the butter, egg, vanilla, and stevia.
4. Stir in the molasses and milk.
5. Incorporate the flour mixture.
6. Divide into 18 portions and roll into balls.
7. Roll in the Swerve until coated.
8. Place on a lined baking sheet.
9. Sprinkle with Swerve and bake for 10 minutes.
10. Allow to cool, then serve.

Serves: **16**

Prep Time: **10** Minutes

Cook Time: **60** Minutes

Total Time: **70** Minutes

INGREDIENTS

- **4 cups rice cereal**
- **2 tbs dark chocolate**
- **2/3 cup honey**
- **½ cup peanut butter**
- **Salt**
- **1 tsp vanilla**

DIRECTIONS

1. Combine all of the ingredients except for the dark chocolate in a bowl.
2. Spread the mixture on a lined baking pan.
3. Drizzle the melted chocolate on top.
4. Refrigerate for 1 hour.
5. Cut into bars and serve.

Serves:	**8-12**	
Prep Time:	**5**	Minutes
Cook Time:	**15**	Minutes
Total Time:	**20**	Minutes

INGREDIENTS

- 1 cup rolled oats
- ¼ cup applesauce
- ½ tsp vanilla extract
- 3 tablespoons chocolate chips
- 2 tablespoons dried fruits
- 1 tsp cinnamon

DIRECTIONS

1. Preheat the oven to 325 F
2. In a bowl combine all ingredients together and mix well
3. Scoop cookies using an ice cream scoop
4. Place cookies onto a prepared baking sheet
5. Place in the oven for 12-15 minutes or until the cookies are done
6. When ready remove from the oven and serve

TANGERINE SMOOTHIE

Serves: **1**

Prep Time: **5**   Minutes

Cook Time: **5**   Minutes

Total Time: **10**   Minutes

INGREDIENTS

- 2 tangerines
- 1 cup pineapple
- 1 banana
- 1 cup ice

DIRECTIONS

1. In a blender place all ingredients and blend until smooth
2. Pour smoothie in a glass and serve

Serves: **1**

Prep Time: **10** Minutes

Cook Time: **0** Minutes

Total Time: **10** Minutes

INGREDIENTS

- Ice
- 6 ounces soda water
- 3 lime slices
- 11 mint leaves
- 1 tbs honey

DIRECTIONS

1. Add mint leaves and lime to a glass and muddle with a spoon.
2. Add honey, ice and soda.
3. Stir to combine.
4. Serve garnished with lime and mint.

PEANUT BUTTER SMOOTHIE

Serves: **1**

Prep Time: **5** Minutes

Cook Time: **5** Minutes

Total Time: **10** Minutes

INGREDIENTS

- 1 cup strawberries
- 1 banana
- 2 tablespoons peanut butter

DIRECTIONS

1. In a blender place all ingredients and blend until smooth
2. Pour smoothie in a glass and serve

CARROT SMOOTHIE

Serves: *1*

Prep Time: *5*   Minutes

Cook Time: *5*   Minutes

Total Time: *10*   Minutes

INGREDIENTS

- 1 carrot
- 1 mango
- 2 tablespoons coconut flakes

DIRECTIONS

1. In a blender place all ingredients and blend until smooth
2. Pour smoothie in a glass and serve

GINGER SMOOTHIE

Serves: *1*

Prep Time: 5   Minutes

Cook Time: 5   Minutes

Total Time: *10* Minutes

INGREDIENTS

- 2 cups pineapple
- 2 tablespoons lime juice
- 1-pice ginger

DIRECTIONS

1. In a blender place all ingredients and blend until smooth
2. Pour smoothie in a glass and serve

KALE SMOOTHIE

Serves: *1*
Prep Time: 5   Minutes

Cook Time: 5   Minutes

Total Time: *10*   Minutes

INGREDIENTS

- 1 cup kale
- 1 cup cherries
- 1 cup blueberries

DIRECTIONS

1. In a blender place all ingredients and blend until smooth
2. Pour smoothie in a glass and serve

MANGO SMOOTHIE

Serves: *1*

Prep Time: 5   Minutes

Cook Time: 5   Minutes

Total Time: *10*   Minutes

INGREDIENTS

- 1 cup mango
- 1 cup cherries
- 1 cup Greek yogurt

DIRECTIONS

1. In a blender place all ingredients and blend until smooth
2. Pour smoothie in a glass and serve

MUFFINS

SIMPLE MUFFINS

Serves: **8-12**

Prep Time: **10**   Minutes

Cook Time: **20**   Minutes

Total Time: **30**   Minutes

INGREDIENTS

- 2 eggs
- 1 tablespoon olive oil
- 1 cup milk
- 2 cups whole wheat flour
- 1 tsp baking soda
- ¼ tsp baking soda
- 1 cup pumpkin puree
- 1 tsp cinnamon
- ¼ cup molasses

DIRECTIONS

1. In a bowl combine all wet ingredients
2. In another bowl combine all dry ingredients

3. Combine wet and dry ingredients together
4. Pour mixture into 8-12 prepared muffin cups, fill 2/3 of the cups
5. Bake for 18-20 minutes at 375 F
6. When ready remove from the oven and serve

Serves: *4*
Prep Time: *10*   Minutes

Cook Time: *20*   Minutes

Total Time: *30*   Minutes

INGREDIENTS

- 1 cup whole-wheat flour
- 1 can of Whole Kernel Corn 15 oz.
- ½ cup milk
- 1 egg
- ½ cup butter
- 1 tablespoon honey
- 1 tablespoon baking powder
- 1 tsp salt

DIRECTIONS

1. Preheat oven to 375 F
2. Blend corn until smooth
3. In a bowl mix baking powder, salt and flour
4. In another bowl mix eggs, butter, corn, milk and honey
5. Pour over the flour mixture and mix well
6. Pour mixture into a cupcake pan and bake for 15-20 minutes

MORNING MUFFINS

Serves: *8-12*

Prep Time: **10**   Minutes

Cook Time: **25**   Minutes

Total Time: **35**   Minutes

INGREDIENTS

- 1 cup oats
- ¼ cup unsweetened applesauce
- 2 egg whites
- 1 cup oat milk
- 1 cup whole wheat flour
- ¼ cup brown sugar
- ¼ tsp baking soda
- ¼ tsp salt
- 1 tsp cinnamon
- ½ cup blueberries

DIRECTIONS

1. Preheat oven to 375 F
2. In a bowl combine all ingredients together and mix well
3. Fill 8-12 paper muffin cups with batter and fold in blueberries
4. Bake for 20-25 minutes, serve when ready

FIBER MUFFINS

Serves: *8-12*

Prep Time: *5*   Minutes

Cook Time: *15*   Minutes

Total Time: *20*   Minutes

INGREDIENTS

- 1 cup wheat bran
- 1cup nonfat milk
- ¼ cup unsweetened applesauce
- 1 egg
- ¼ cup brown sugar
- ¼ cup all-purpose flour
- ¼ cup whole wheat flour
- 1 tsp baking powder
- 1 tsp baking soda
- ¼ tsp salt
- 1 cup blueberries

DIRECTIONS

1. Preheat oven to 400 F
2. In a bowl combine wheat bran and milk and set aside
3. In another bowl combine egg, brown sugar, apple sauce and stir in bran mixture, mix well

4. In another bowl combine baking soda, baking powder, wheat flour, all-purpose flour and mix well

5. Stir flour mixture into bran and egg mixture and mix well

6. Fold in blueberries and fill muffin cups with batter

7. Bake for 12-15 minutes

8. When ready remove and serve

Serves: **8-12**
Prep Time: **10** Minutes

Cook Time: **20** Minutes

Total Time: **30** Minutes

INGREDIENTS

- 2 eggs
- 1 tablespoon olive oil
- 1 cup milk
- 2 cups whole wheat flour
- 1 tsp baking soda
- ¼ tsp baking soda
- 1 tsp cinnamon
- 1 cup strawberries

DIRECTIONS

1. In a bowl combine all wet ingredients
2. In another bowl combine all dry ingredients
3. Combine wet and dry ingredients together
4. Fold in strawberries and mix well
5. Pour mixture into 8-12 prepared muffin cups, fill 2/3 of the cups
6. Bake for 18-20 minutes at 375 F, remove when ready

CHOCOLATE MUFFINS

Serves: **8-12**
Prep Time: **10**   Minutes

Cook Time: **20**   Minutes

Total Time: **30**   Minutes

INGREDIENTS

- 2 eggs
- 1 tablespoon olive oil
- 1 cup milk
- 2 cups whole wheat flour
- 1 tsp baking soda
- ¼ tsp baking soda
- 1 tsp cinnamon
- 1 cup chocolate chips

DIRECTIONS

1. In a bowl combine all wet ingredients
2. In another bowl combine all dry ingredients
3. Combine wet and dry ingredients together
4. Fold in chocolate chips and mix well
5. Pour mixture into 8-12 prepared muffin cups, fill 2/3 of the cups
6. Bake for 18-20 minutes at 375 F, remove when ready

SIMPLE MUFFINS

Serves:	*8-12*
Prep Time:	*10* Minutes
Cook Time:	*20* Minutes
Total Time:	*30* Minutes

INGREDIENTS

- 2 eggs
- 1 tablespoon olive oil
- 1 cup milk
- 2 cups whole wheat flour
- 1 tsp baking soda
- ¼ tsp baking soda
- 1 tsp cinnamon

DIRECTIONS

1. In a bowl combine all wet ingredients
2. In another bowl combine all dry ingredients
3. Combine wet and dry ingredients together
4. Pour mixture into 8-12 prepared muffin cups, fill 2/3 of the cups
5. Bake for 18-20 minutes at 375 F
6. When ready remove from the oven and serve

THIRD COOKBOOK

SIDE DISHES

MINESTRONE SOUP

Serves: **6**

Prep Time: **10**   Minutes

Cook Time: **50**   Minutes

Total Time: **60**   Minutes

INGREDIENTS

- 2 onions
- 1 cup peas
- 1 can tomatoes
- 2 cups tomato sauce
- 3 carrots
- 1 cup green beans
- 2 tbs basil
- 6 cups water
- 2 cloves garlic
- Salt
- 2 tbs cheese
- 1.5 cups kidney
- 2 cups celery
- 1 bell pepper

DIRECTIONS

1. Put the onions, celery and carrots into a pot of water.

2. Add the green beans, peas, tomatoes and bell pepper when the water starts to boil, then allow to boil for 30 minutes.

3. Add the tomato sauce and basil then season with salt.

4. Allow to simmer for 10 minutes, then add the garlic and simmer for 5 more minutes.

5. Serve topped with cheese.

TUNA SALAD

Serves: **4**

Prep Time: **10** Minutes

Cook Time: **5** Minutes

Total Time: **15** Minutes

INGREDIENTS
- ½ tsp lemon zest
- Salt
- Pepper
- 4 eggs
- 1/3 red onion
- ¾ lb green beans
- 1 can tuna
- 1 tsp oregano
- 6 tbs olive oil
- 3 tbs lemon juice
- 1 can beans
- 1 can black olives

DIRECTIONS

1. Place the green beans, 1/3 cup water and salt to taste in a skillet.
2. Bring to a boil, covered.
3. Cook for 5 minutes.

4. Dump them onto a lined cookie sheet.

5. Mix the white beans, onion, olives and tuna.

6. Combine the oregano, lemon juice and zest, and oil in a separate bowl.

7. Pour the mixture over the tuna mixture.

8. Season and serve immediately with the boiled eggs.

CHICKEN SKILLET

Serves: *4*
Prep Time: *10* Minutes

Cook Time: *30* Minutes

Total Time: *40* Minutes

INGREDIENTS

- 1 tsp oil
- ½ cup carrots
- 1 zucchini
- 1 bell pepper
- ½ lb chicken
- 1 onion

DIRECTIONS

1. Cut the chicken into strips, then cook in the oil until it gets brown.
2. Remove from the skillet and add the vegetables.
3. Cook until soft for 10 minutes, then add the chicken.
4. Season and serve immediately.

SPINACH QUESADILLAS

Serves: **4**

Prep Time: **10**   Minutes

Cook Time: **15**   Minutes

Total Time: **25**   Minutes

INGREDIENTS

- **4 cups spinach**
- **4 green onions**
- **1 tomato**
- **½ lemon juice**
- **1 tsp cumin**
- **1 tsp garlic powder**
- **Salt**
- **1 cup cheese**
- **4 tortillas**

DIRECTIONS

1. Cook all of the ingredients except for the cheese and tortillas in a skillet.
2. Cook until the spinach is wilted.
3. Remove to a bowl and add the cheese.
4. Place the mixture on half of the tortilla, fold the other half and cook for 2 minutes on each side on a griddle

Serves: **4**
Prep Time: **10** Minutes

Cook Time: **0** Minutes

Total Time: **10** Minutes

INGREDIENTS

- 1 can garbanzo beans
- 1 can red beans
- 1 tomato
- ½ red onion
- ½ lemon juice
- 1 tbs olive oil

DIRECTIONS

1. Mix all of the ingredients together in a bowl.
2. Season with salt and serve immediately.

GARLIC SALMON

Serves: **4**

Prep Time: **10** Minutes

Cook Time: **20** Minutes

Total Time: **30** Minutes

INGREDIENTS

- 2 lb salmon
- 2 tbs water
- Salt
- 2 tbs parsley
- 4 cloves garlic

DIRECTIONS

1. Preheat the oven to 400F.
2. Mix the garlic, parsley, salt and water in a bowl.
3. Brush the mixture over the salmon.
4. Place the fish on a baking tray and cover with aluminum foil.
5. Cook for 20 minutes.
6. Serve with vegetables.

TUNA WRAP

Serves:	**4**	
Prep Time:	**10**	Minutes
Cook Time:	**0**	Minutes
Total Time:	**10**	Minutes

INGREDIENTS

- 6 ounces tuna
- 2 tsp yogurt
- ½ celery stalk
- Handful baby spinach
- ½ onion
- 2 tsp lemon juice
- 4 tortillas

DIRECTIONS

1. Mix all of the ingredients except for the tortillas in a bowl.
2. Spread the mixture over the tortillas, then wrap them up.
3. Serve immediately.

ROASTED CHICKEN WRAP

Serves: **4**

Prep Time: **10**   Minutes

Cook Time: **10**   Minutes

Total Time: **20**   Minutes

INGREDIENTS

- **1 cup chicken breast**
- **2 tsp yogurt**
- **1/3 cup celery**
- **8 tomato slices**
- **½ onion**
- **1 tbs mustard**
- **2 tbs ketchup**
- **4 tortillas**

DIRECTIONS

1. Cut the chicken as you desire and grill until done on each side.
2. Mix all of the ingredients except for the tortillas in a bowl.
3. Spread the mixture over the tortillas and add the chicken.
4. Serve immediately.

LENTIL SALAD

Serves: *4*

Prep Time: *10*   Minutes

Cook Time: *0*   Minutes

Total Time: *10*   Minutes

INGREDIENTS

- 1 cup cooked lentils
- 1 cup baby spinach
- 1 poached egg
- ¼ avocado
- ½ tomato
- 1-2 slices whole wheat bread

DIRECTIONS

1. Mix all of the ingredients together except for the bread.
2. Toast the bread.
3. Serve immediately together.

STUFFED EGGPLANT

Serves: **4**

Prep Time: **10**   Minutes

Cook Time: **50**   Minutes

Total Time: **60**   Minutes

INGREDIENTS
- 1 eggplant
- 2 onions
- 1 red pepper
- ½ cup tomato juice
- ¼ cup cheese

DIRECTIONS

1. Preheat the oven to 350F.
2. Cut the eggplant in half and cook for 30 minutes.
3. Cook the diced onion in 2 tbs of water until brown.
4. Add the pepper and add it to the onion, cooking for another 5 minutes.
5. Add the tomato juice and allow to cook for another 5 minutes.
6. Scoop out the eggplant.
7. Mix the eggplant with the onion mixture, then add it back into the eggplant shell.
8. Grate the cheese on top and bake for another 10 minutes.
9. Serve hot.

Serves: 2

Prep Time: 5   Minutes

Cook Time: 20 Minutes

Total Time: 25 Minutes

INGREDIENTS

- 1 tbs olive oil
- ¼ tsp thyme
- 1 cup arugula
- ½ lemon juice
- 1 head broccoli
- 1 clove garlic
- 2 cups water
- ¼ tsp salt
- ¼ tsp black pepper
- ½ yellow onion

DIRECTIONS

1. Heat the oil in a saucepan.
2. Cook the onion until soft, then add the garlic and cook for another minute.
3. Add the broccoli and cook for 5 minutes.
4. Add the water, thyme, salt, and pepper.

5. Bring to boil, then lower the heat and cook for 10 minutes.
6. Transfer to a blender, blend, then add the arugula and blend until smooth.
7. Add the lemon juice and serve immediately.

Serves: **4**

Prep Time: **20**   Minutes

Cook Time: **25**   Minutes

Total Time: **45**   Minutes

INGREDIENTS

- ½ onion
- 1 cup mushrooms
- ½ yellow bell pepper
- 1 cup spinach
- 1 can tomatoes
- 1 tbs tomato paste
- 4 red bell peppers
- 1 lb ground turkey
- 2 tbs olive oil
- 1 zucchini
- ½ green bell pepper
- 1 tsp Italian seasoning
- ½ tsp garlic powder
- Salt
- Pepper

DIRECTIONS

1. Bring a pot of water to a boil.
2. Cut the tops off the peppers, and remove the seeds.
3. Cook in water for 5 minutes.
4. Preheat the oven to 350F.
5. Cook the turkey until brown.
6. Heat the oil and cook the onion, mushrooms, zucchini, green and yellow pepper, and spinach until soft.
7. Add the turkey and the rest of the ingredients.
8. Stuff the peppers with the mixture.
9. Bake for 15 minutes.
10. Serve hot.

POTATO SALAD

Serves: **6**
Prep Time: **5**   Minutes

Cook Time: **10**   Minutes

Total Time: **15**   Minutes

INGREDIENTS

- 1 red onion
- 2 tsp cumin seeds
- 1 cloves garlic
- ½ cup olive oil
- 4 potatoes
- ½ cup lemon juice
- 2 tbs fresh parsley
- 1 ½ tsp salt
- 2 tsp turmeric powder

DIRECTIONS

1. Steam the potatoes for 10 minutes, until tender.
2. Mix the lemon juice, turmeric, cumin seeds, and salt.
3. Place the potatoes in a bowl and pour the mixture over.
4. Add the onion and garlic and stir to coat.
5. Refrigerate until the potatoes are cold.

6. Add olive oil and herbs and stir.

Serves: **4**

Prep Time: **20** Minutes

Cook Time: **10** Minutes

Total Time: **30** Minutes

INGREDIENTS

- **1 cucumber**
- **1 cup red cabbage**
- **1 ½ lbs ground pork**
- **6 radishes**
- **4 tsp sugar**
- **2 tbs olive oil**
- **¼ cup white wine vinegar**
- **2 tbs soy sauce**
- **2 tsp garlic powder**
- **2 tbs sesame oil**
- **4 scallions**
- **2 tsp Sriracha**
- **12 tortillas**
- **2 tsp cilantro**
- **½ cup sour cream**
- **Salt**
- **Pepper**

DIRECTIONS

1. Place the cucumbers, radishes, vinegar, 2 tsp sugar, salt, and pepper in a bowl.

2. Cook the scallions and cabbage in the oil until soft.

3. Add the pork, garlic powder, and 2 tsp sugar and cook for another 5 minutes.

4. Add the sesame oil, Sriracha, soy sauce and combine.

5. Season with salt and pepper.

6. Heat the tortillas in the microwave for a few seconds.

7. Spread sour cream on the tortilla, add the mixture, sprinkle cilantro over and add the cucumber and radishes.

8. Serve immediately.

Serves: **4**

Prep Time: **10** Minutes

Cook Time: **25** Minutes

Total Time: **40** Minutes

INGREDIENTS

- 1 lb. ground lamb
- 1 egg
- 1 cloves garlic
- 1 handful parsley
- 1 tablespoon dried oregano
- 1 tsp dried rosemary
- ½ cup fetta cheese
- ¼ tsp salt

DIRECTIONS

1. Preheat the oven to 325 F
2. In a bowl mix all ingredients
3. Form into meat balls
4. Bake for 20-25 minutes, remove and serve

BAKED CHILLI CHICKEN

Serves: **4**

Prep Time: **10** Minutes

Cook Time: **30** Minutes

Total Time: **40** Minutes

INGREDIENTS

- 2 lb. chicken drumsticks
- 3 tablespoons olive oil
- 2 cloves garlic
- 2 tablespoons lime juice
- 3 tsp lime zest
- 1 tsp chilli flakes
- salt

DIRECTIONS

1. In a bowl place all ingredients except chicken drumsticks
2. Refrigerate and then add the drumsticks for 1-2 hours
3. Preheat oven to 350 F
4. Arrange the chicken drumsticks on a greased oven tray and bake for 40-45 minutes
5. Remove and serve

Serves: 2
Prep Time: **10**   Minutes

Cook Time: **15**   Minutes

Total Time: **25**   Minutes

INGREDIENTS

- 1 head broccoli
- 1 handful cashews
- 1 tablespoons macadamia nut oil
- 2 tablespoons coconut aminos
- 1 tablespoon fish sauce
- 2 cloves garlic
- ¼ red pepper
- 1 tablespoon lime juice
- 6 oz. shrimp
- 1 tablespoon sesame seeds
- salt

DIRECTIONS

1. In a frying pan heat oil over medium heat
2. Add garlic, sesame seeds, red pepper and cashews
3. Add shrimp and fry for 3-4 minutes

4. Remove and serve

SPINACH FRITATTA

Serves: **2**
Prep Time: **10**   Minutes

Cook Time: **20**   Minutes

Total Time: **30**   Minutes

INGREDIENTS

- ½ lb. spinach
- 1 tablespoon olive oil
- ½ red onion
- 2 eggs
- ¼ tsp salt
- 2 oz. cheddar cheese
- 1 garlic clove
- ¼ tsp dill

DIRECTIONS

1. In a bowl whisk eggs with salt and cheese
2. In a frying pan heat olive oil and pour egg mixture
3. Add remaining ingredients and mix well
4. Serve when ready

TURNIP FRITATTA

Serves: **2**

Prep Time: **10** Minutes

Cook Time: **20** Minutes

Total Time: **30** Minutes

INGREDIENTS

- ½ lb. spinach
- ¼ cup turnip
- ½ red onion
- 2 eggs
- ¼ tsp salt
- 2 oz. cheddar cheese
- 1 garlic clove
- ¼ tsp dill

DIRECTIONS

1. In a bowl whisk eggs with salt and cheese
2. In a frying pan heat olive oil and pour egg mixture
3. Add remaining ingredients and mix well
4. Serve when ready

SQUASH FRITATTA

Serves: **2**
Prep Time: **10** Minutes
Cook Time: **20** Minutes
Total Time: **30** Minutes

INGREDIENTS

- 1 cup squash
- 1 tablespoon olive oil
- ½ red onion
- 2 eggs
- ¼ tsp salt
- 2 oz. cheddar cheese
- 1 garlic clove
- ¼ tsp dill

DIRECTIONS

1. In a bowl whisk eggs with salt and cheese
2. In a frying pan heat olive oil and pour egg mixture
3. Add remaining ingredients and mix well
4. Serve when ready

HAM FRITATTA

Serves: **2**
Prep Time: **10** Minutes

Cook Time: **20** Minutes

Total Time: **30** Minutes

INGREDIENTS

- 8-10 slices ham
- 1 tablespoon olive oil
- ½ red onion
- 2 eggs
- ¼ tsp salt
- 2 oz. parmesan cheese
- 1 garlic clove
- ¼ tsp dill

DIRECTIONS

1. In a bowl whisk eggs with salt and parmesan cheese
2. In a frying pan heat olive oil and pour egg mixture
3. Add remaining ingredients and mix well
4. When prosciutto and eggs are cooked remove from heat and serve

ONION FRITATTA

Serves: **2**
Prep Time: **10**   Minutes

Cook Time: **20**   Minutes

Total Time: **30**   Minutes

INGREDIENTS

- 1 tablespoon olive oil
- ½ red onion
- 2 eggs
- ¼ tsp salt
- 2 oz. cheddar cheese
- 1 garlic clove
- ¼ tsp dill

DIRECTIONS

1. In a bowl whisk eggs with salt and cheese
2. In a frying pan heat olive oil and pour egg mixture
3. Add remaining ingredients and mix well
4. Serve when ready

FRIED CHICKEN WITH ALMONDS

Serves:　　　2

Prep Time:　**10**　Minutes

Cook Time:　**25**　Minutes

Total Time:　**35**　Minutes

INGREDIENTS

- 1 cup bread crumbs
- ¼ cup parmesan cheese
- ¼ cup almonds
- 1 tsp salt
- 1 tablespoon parley leaves
- 1 clove garlic
- ½ cup olive oil
- 2 lb. chicken breast

DIRECTIONS

1. In a bowl combine parsley, almonds, garlic, parmesan, bread crumbs, salt and mix well
2. In a bowl add olive oil and dip chicken breast into olive oil
3. Place chicken into the breadcrumb mixture and toss to coat
4. Bake chicken at 375 F for 20-25 minutes
5. When ready remove chicken from the oven and serve

FILET MIGNON WITH TOMATO SAUCE

Serves: **4**

Prep Time: **10**   Minutes

Cook Time: **30**   Minutes

Total Time: **40**   Minutes

INGREDIENTS

- 1 tsp soy sauce
- 1 tsp mustard
- 1 tsp parsley leaves
- 1 clove garlic
- 2-3 tomatoes
- 2 tsp olive oil
- 4-5 beef tenderloin steaks
- ½ tsp salt

DIRECTIONS

1. In a bowl combine parsley, garlic, soy sauce, mustard and mix well
2. Stir in tomatoes slices and toss to coat
3. In a skillet heat olive oil and place the steak
4. Cook until golden brown for 3-4 minutes
5. Transfer skillet to the oven and bake at 375 F for 8-10 minutes
6. When ready remove and serve with tomato sauce

ZUCCHINI NOODLES

Serves: *1*

Prep Time: *5* Minutes

Cook Time: *15* Minutes

Total Time: *20* Minutes

INGREDIENTS

- 2 zucchinis
- 1 tablespoon olive oil
- 1 garlic clove
- ½ cup parmesan cheese
- 1 tsp salt

DIRECTIONS

1. Spiralize zucchini and set aside
2. In a skillet melt butter, add garlic and zucchini noodles
3. Toss to coat and cook for 5-6 minutes
4. When ready remove from the skillet and serve with parmesan cheese on top

Serves: **4**

Prep Time: **10** Minutes

Cook Time: **15** Minutes

Total Time: **25** Minutes

INGREDIENTS

- 1 cup water
- 1 lb. green beans
- 2 tomatoes
- 1 tsp olive oil
- 1 tsp Italian dressing
- salt

DIRECTIONS

1. In a pot bring water to a boil
2. Add green beans, tomatoes and boil for 10-12 minutes
3. Remove green beans and tomatoes to a bowl
4. Chop tomatoes, add Italian dressing, olive oil and serve

ROASTED CAULIFLOWER RICE

Serves: 2

Prep Time: *10* Minutes

Cook Time: 25 Minutes

Total Time: 35 Minutes

INGREDIENTS

- 3-4 cups frozen cauliflower rice
- 1 tablespoon olive oil
- 2 garlic cloves
- ½ cup parmesan cheese

DIRECTIONS

1. Place the cauliflower rice on a sheet pan
2. Sprinkle garlic and olive oil over the cauliflower rice and toss well
3. Spread cauliflower rice in a single layer in the pan
4. Roast cauliflower rice at 375 F for 20-25 minutes
5. When ready remove from the oven and serve with parmesan cheese on top

ROASTED SQUASH

Serves: **3-4**
Prep Time: **10** Minutes

Cook Time: **20** Minutes

Total Time: **30** Minutes

INGREDIENTS

- 2 delicata squashes
- 2 tablespoons olive oil
- 1 tsp curry powder
- 1 tsp salt

DIRECTIONS

1. Preheat the oven to 400 F
2. Cut everything in half lengthwise
3. Toss everything with olive oil and place onto a prepared baking sheet
4. Roast for 18-20 minutes at 400 F or until golden brown
5. When ready remove from the oven and serve

BRUSSELS SPROUT CHIPS

Serves: **2**
Prep Time: **10** Minutes

Cook Time: **20** Minutes

Total Time: **30** Minutes

INGREDIENTS

- 1 lb. brussels sprouts
- 1 tablespoon olive oil
- 1 tablespoon parmesan cheese
- 1 tsp garlic powder
- 1 tsp seasoning

DIRECTIONS

1. Preheat the oven to 425 F
2. In a bowl toss everything with olive oil and seasoning
3. Spread everything onto a prepared baking sheet
4. Bake for 8-10 minutes or until crisp
5. When ready remove from the oven and serve

SQUASH CHIPS

Serves: **2**

Prep Time: **10** Minutes

Cook Time: **20** Minutes

Total Time: **30** Minutes

INGREDIENTS

- 1 lb. squash
- 1 tablespoon olive oil
- 1 tsp garlic powder
- 1 tsp seasoning

DIRECTIONS

1. Preheat the oven to 425 F
2. In a bowl toss everything with olive oil and seasoning
3. Spread everything onto a prepared baking sheet
4. Bake for 8-10 minutes or until crisp
5. When ready remove from the oven and serve

ZUCCHINI CHIPS

Serves: **2**

Prep Time: **10**   Minutes

Cook Time: **20**   Minutes

Total Time: **30**   Minutes

INGREDIENTS

- 1 lb. zucchini
- 1 tablespoon olive oil
- 1 tablespoon parmesan cheese
- 1 tsp garlic powder
- 1 tsp seasoning

DIRECTIONS

1. Preheat the oven to 425 F
2. In a bowl toss everything with olive oil and seasoning
3. Spread everything onto a prepared baking sheet
4. Bake for 8-10 minutes or until crisp
5. When ready remove from the oven and serve

CARROT CHIPS

Serves: 2
Prep Time: 10 Minutes

Cook Time: 20 Minutes

Total Time: 30 Minutes

INGREDIENTS

- 1 lb. carrot
- 1 tablespoon olive oil
- 1 tablespoon parmesan cheese
- 1 tsp garlic powder
- 1 tsp seasoning

DIRECTIONS

1. Preheat the oven to 425 F
2. In a bowl toss everything with olive oil and seasoning
3. Spread everything onto a prepared baking sheet
4. Bake for 8-10 minutes or until crisp
5. When ready remove from the oven and serve

PASTA

SIMPLE SPAGHETTI

Serves: 2
Prep Time: 5   Minutes

Cook Time: 15   Minutes

Total Time: 20   Minutes

INGREDIENTS

- 10 oz. spaghetti
- 2 eggs
- ½ cup parmesan cheese
- 1 tsp black pepper
- Olive oil
- 1 tsp parsley
- 2 cloves garlic

DIRECTIONS

1. In a pot boil spaghetti (or any other type of pasta), drain and set aside
2. In a bowl whish eggs with parmesan cheese
3. In a skillet heat olive oil, add garlic and cook for 1-2 minutes
4. Pour egg mixture and mix well
5. Add pasta and stir well

6. When ready garnish with parsley and serve

ARTICHOKE PASTA

Serves: 2
Prep Time: 5   Minutes

Cook Time: 15   Minutes

Total Time: 20   Minutes

INGREDIENTS

- ¼ cup olive oil
- 1 jar artichokes
- 2 cloves garlic
- 1 tablespoon thyme leaves
- 1 lb. pasta
- 2 tablespoons butter
- 1. Cup basil
- ½ cup parmesan cheese

DIRECTIONS

1. In a pot boil spaghetti (or any other type of pasta), drain and set aside
2. Place all the ingredients for the sauce in a pot and bring to a simmer
3. Add pasta and mix well
4. When ready garnish with parmesan cheese and serve

CHICKEN PASTA

Serves: 2

Prep Time: 5   Minutes

Cook Time: 15   Minutes

Total Time: 20   Minutes

INGREDIENTS

- 1 lb. cooked chicken breast
- 8 oz. pasta
- 2 tablespoons butter
- 1 tablespoon garlic
- 1 tablespoon flour
- ½ cup milk
- ½ cup heavy cream
- 1 jar red bell peppers
- 2 tablespoons basil

DIRECTIONS

1. In a pot boil spaghetti (or any other type of pasta), drain and set aside
2. Place all the ingredients for the sauce in a pot and bring to a simmer
3. Add pasta and mix well
4. When ready garnish with parmesan cheese and serve

SALAD RECIPES

MEDITERRANEAN TUNA SALAD

Serves: **4**

Prep Time: **10** Minutes

Cook Time: **30** Minutes

Total Time: **40** Minutes

INGREDIENTS

- 2 cans tuna
- 2 celery stalks
- 1 cucumber
- 4 radishes
- 2 onions
- 1 red onion
- ¼ Kalamata olives
- 1 bunch parsley
- 10 mint leaves
- 1 tomato
- 1 serving mustard vinaigrette

DIRECTIONS

1. In a bowl combine all ingredients together
2. Add salad dressing and serve

Serves: 2

Prep Time: 5   Minutes

Cook Time: 5   Minutes

Total Time: 10 Minutes

INGREDIENTS

- 2 cans tuna
- 1 red bell pepper
- 1 can black beans
- 1 can black olives
- 1 can yellow corn
- 2 tomatoes
- 2 avocados

DRESSING

- ½ cup Greek yogurt
- ¼ cup mayonnaise
- 1 tsp garlic powder
- ¼ tsp cumin

DIRECTIONS

1. In a bowl combine all ingredients together
2. In another bowl combine all ingredients for the dressing

3. Add dressing, mix well and serve

Serves: **4**

Prep Time: **10** Minutes

Cook Time: **10** Minutes

Total Time: **20** Minutes

INGREDIENTS

- ¼ lbs. noodle
- ¼ lbs. baby spinach
- 3 oz. cooked prawn
- ¼ lbs. snap pea
- 1 carrot

DRESSING

- 1 red chili
- 1 tsp fish sauce
- 1 tablespoon mint
- 2 tablespoons rice vinegar
- 1 tsp sugar

DIRECTIONS

1. In a bowl add all dressing ingredients and mix well
2. In another bowl add salad ingredients and mix well, pour dressing over salad and serve

ARUGULA AND SWEET POTATO SALAD

Serves: **2**

Prep Time: **10** Minutes

Cook Time: **15** Minutes

Total Time: **25** Minutes

INGREDIENTS

- 1 lb. sweet potatoes
- 1 cup walnuts
- 1 tablespoon olive oil
- 1 cup water
- 1 tablespoon soy sauce
- 3 cups arugula

DIRECTIONS

1. Bake potatoes at 400 F until tender, remove and set aside
2. In a bowl drizzle, walnuts with olive oil and microwave for 2-3 minutes or until toasted
3. In a bowl combine all salad ingredients and mix well
4. Pour over soy sauce and serve

Serves: **4**

Prep Time: **10**   Minutes

Cook Time: **30**   Minutes

Total Time: **40**   Minutes

INGREDIENTS

- 2 mangoes
- Juice of 1 lemon
- ¼ onion
- 1 tablespoon cilantro laves

DIRECTIONS

1. In a bowl combine all salad ingredients and mix well
2. Add salad dressing and serve when ready

COUSCOUS SALAD

Serves: **4**

Prep Time: **10** Minutes

Cook Time: **30** Minutes

Total Time: **40** Minutes

INGREDIENTS

- 1 cup couscous
- 1 cup zucchini
- 1 red bell pepper
- ¼ cup red onion
- ¼ tsp cumin
- ¼ tsp black pepper
- ¼ cup salad dressing
- ¼ tsp parsley

DIRECTIONS

1. In a bowl combine all salad ingredients and mix well
2. Add salad dressing and serve when ready

Serves: *4*

Prep Time: *10* Minutes

Cook Time: *30* Minutes

Total Time: *40* Minutes

INGREDIENTS

- 1 oz. red potatoes
- 1 package green beans
- 2 eggs
- ½ cup tomatoes
- 2 tablespoons wine vinegar
- ¼ tsp salt
- ½ tsp pepper
- ½ tsp thyme
- ¼ cup olive oil
- 6 oz. tuna
- ¼ cup Kalamata olives

DIRECTIONS

1. In a bowl combine all ingredients together
2. Add salad dressing and serve

Serves: 2

Prep Time: **10**   Minutes

Cook Time: **30**   Minutes

Total Time: **40**   Minutes

INGREDIENTS

- ¼ cup lemon juice
- ¼ cup rice wine vinegar
- 1 tsp sugar
- 1 cucumber
- ¼ cup mint
- 10 oz. cooked crab
- 2 cups mixed salad greens
- 2 lime wedges

DIRECTIONS

1. In a bowl combine all salad ingredients and mix well
2. Add salad dressing and serve when ready

THANK YOU FOR READING THIS BOOK!

9 781664 044449